A Plague of a Divorce

By

Catherine Matthews-Hyatt

First published in the United States in 2025 by TTRP

© The Throne Room Publisher US, 2025

Text copyright © Catherine Matthews-Hyatt, 2025

Cover illustration and design © The Throne Room Publisher US

The moral rights of the author have been asserted

All rights reserved

No part of this publication maybe reproduced, stored in a retrieval system or transmitted in any form or by any means, without the prior permission in writing of the publisher, nor be otherwise circulated in any form of binding or cover other than that in which it is published and without a similar condition including this condition being imposed on the subsequent purchaser.

All biblical references and teachings within this book are shared with the purpose of spiritual growth, encouragement, and personal reflection. This work is not intended to replace professional counseling, legal advice, or pastoral care but to inspire readers toward healing and restoration through faith in Jesus Christ.

Unless otherwise indicated, all Scripture quotations are taken from the Holy Bible, New International Version® (NIV), copyright © 1973, 1978, 1984, 2011 by Biblica, Inc.™ Used by permission. All rights reserved worldwide. Scripture quotations marked (KJV) are taken from the Holy Bible, King James Version, public domain.

Printed in the United States of America

https://www.thethroneroom.co/

Our books may be purchased in bulk for promotional, educational, spiritual speaker or business use.

Please contact The Throne Room Publishers at +1-702-479-7691, or by email at order@thethroneroom.co

First Edition November 2025

ISBN: 979-8-9936739-1-2 (Paperback)

Dedication

To my Lord and Savior, Jesus Christ,

With all my heart, I dedicate this book to You, the One who sustained me through the storm, held me in the midnight hour, and turned my pain into purpose. Through the trials of divorce, You revealed Yourself to me in ways I had never known. You gave me wisdom beyond my understanding, strength in my weakness, and insight that only comes from walking through the fire with You.

What the enemy meant for evil, You turned for my good. In the breaking, You rebuilt me. In the loss, You became my greatest gain. In the silence of loneliness, I heard Your voice more clearly. Through every tear, every battle, and every shattered dream, You were there, shaping me, refining me, and drawing me deeper into Your presence.

"For He knows the way that I take; when He has tested me, I will come forth as gold."
— *Job 23:10*

This book is a monument to Your faithfulness, a witness to the power of Your healing, and a declaration that nothing, not even the plague of divorce, can separate me from Your love. Thank You for making beauty from ashes.

Your Daughter Forever,
Prophetess Catherine Matthews

Table of Contents

A Note for Readers..1

Chapter 1 The Plague of Water Turned to Blood: The Beginning of the End 3

Chapter 2 The Plague of Frogs: Chaos and Confusion........9

Chapter 3 The Plague of Lice – Internal Struggles and Hidden Sins 15

Chapter 4 The Plague of Flies – Swarmed by Chaos.........21

Chapter 5 The Plague of Livestock – Losing What Sustained Me 27

Chapter 6 The Plague of Boils – Pain That Won't Heal 35

Chapter 7 The Plague of Hail – Shattered Dreams 41

Chapter 8 The Plague of Locusts – Devouring What Remained 49

Chapter 9 The Plague of Darkness – Lost in the Shadows 57

Chapter 10 The Plague of the Death of the Firstborn – Dying to Myself 65

Conclusion From Plague to Purpose..................................72

About the Author..77

A Note for Readers

Dear Reader,

If you are holding this book, you may be walking through, or still healing from, a storm you never expected. I want you to know: *I see you*. More importantly, God sees you.

Contrary to popular belief, divorce is not the end of a marriage but rather a journey through pain, loss, and transformation. If you've ever felt the sting of betrayal, the weight of loneliness, or the struggle of rebuilding your life, know this: *you are not alone.*

A Plague of Divorce was born out of my own experiences, nights filled with silent tears, battles in the courtroom, and the deep ache of watching a life once built together slowly crumble. But through it all, I discovered something greater: the unfailing presence of God.

Each chapter in this book mirrors one of the ten plagues of Egypt, drawing a parallel between their devastation and the emotional and spiritual warfare of divorce. Just as God led His people out of bondage, He longs to lead you into healing, freedom, and restoration.

Apart from being a personal story, this book is proof of what God can do when we surrender our brokenness to Him. My prayer is that within these pages, you will find encouragement, strength, and renewed hope.

No matter what you've lost, God can restore it.

No matter how shattered you feel, He can make you whole again.

You are not forgotten, and your story is far from over.

May this book be a light in your darkest moments and a reminder that with God, even after devastation, there is victory.

With love and faith,
Prophetess Catherine Matthews

Chapter 1
The Plague of Water Turned to Blood: The Beginning of the End

The first plague that God brought upon Egypt turned the life-giving Nile River into blood, and hence, what once sustained the people became a source of death and devastation. That's how my marriage began to feel. Something that should have nourished me, brought stability, and produced joy became toxic, draining, and destructive.

From the outside, we looked like the perfect family. I was a Black woman living in a middle-class neighborhood, married with four beautiful children, enrolled in private school. We were active in the church and respected in our community.

But behind closed doors, my reality was bleeding out.

I never married Dwight for love. I married him because I thought it was the "right" thing to do, for the children, for the appearance of a whole family, for the illusion of stability. I believed that by sacrificing my desires, I could protect my children from the pain of a broken home. But in doing so, I ignored the warnings that God had already placed deep in my spirit.

Dwight was never submitted to God. He dismissed my prophetic insight and rejected the spiritual leadership I tried to bring into our home. His heart was hardened, much like Pharaoh's, unyielding, prideful, and resistant to truth.

"But Pharaoh's heart was hard, and he would not listen."
—*Exodus 7:13*

Still, I stayed. I prayed. I hoped. I tried to hold together what was already unraveling. Even as the cracks deepened, I convinced myself that God could fix what was broken. I believed that if I prayed hard enough, fasted long enough, and endured quietly, Dwight would change. But deep down, I already knew that we were drowning.

Then came the betrayal that finally shattered the illusion. Dwight had been unfaithful. He wasn't hiding it; he flaunted it. He spoke about the other woman as if I were the one who had failed him. The worst part of this was that I knew her. That betrayal went beyond infidelity; it cut through every wall of trust that had ever existed between us. It felt like a public crucifixion of my dignity.

I tried to keep my emotions buried. I was a minister. A woman of faith. A mother. I told myself to be strong for the kids and for the church. But on the inside, I was breaking. My faith had always been my anchor, but now I found myself adrift in anger, bitterness, and despair.

The Lord had warned me more than once. He had shown me Dwight's unfaithfulness and the spiritual disconnect in our home. But He had also shown me myself, my pride, my avoidance, my fear.

"For the wages of sin is death, but the gift of God is eternal life in Christ Jesus our Lord."
—*Romans 6:23*

I wanted to blame Dwight entirely, but I had to confront my own choices, too. In my brokenness, I sought comfort in the arms of another man, an ex-boyfriend from years past who had resurfaced in my life at the wrong time. At first, I convinced myself that I deserved it. *If Dwight could shamelessly step outside of our marriage, why shouldn't I?* I thought

But as soon as it happened, guilt hit me like a flood. The Holy Spirit convicted me instantly. I knew better. I had stepped out of the will of God, and I had turned my pain into justification for sin.

> "But whoever denies Me before men, I also will deny before My Father who is in heaven."
> —*Matthew 10:33*

The marriage was already hemorrhaging, but now I had added my own wound to the bleeding. I had hoped the affair would numb the pain. Instead, it deepened it.

What started as a moment of desperation, reaching out to someone who had once made me feel loved, turned into a dangerous escape. It wasn't love. It wasn't healing. It was a reaction to my emptiness.

Dwight's betrayal had broken me, but mine had broken me even more. Because I knew the truth. I knew God. And I had chosen to ignore His voice.

Now, as you reflect on the lessons in this chapter, I encourage you to pause and look inward. Healing doesn't happen by reading alone; it happens through honest reflection and communion with God. The questions below are here to guide you in that process. Take your time. Journal your thoughts. Let the Holy Spirit reveal what still needs healing, release, or realignment in your life. This is more than a story; it's an invitation to transformation.

I am also including a short prayer below, which I will continue to do at the end of every chapter, not as a script, but as a spiritual starting point. Whether you read it quietly or speak it aloud, let it become a doorway to deeper intimacy with God. Invite Him into your chaos, your pain, and your questions. He is not just the God of the story I'm telling; He is the God of the one you are living.

Devotional Prayer

Father,

You are the God who sees, who heals, and who restores. Just as You turned the Nile to blood to reveal what was hidden, turn over the areas in my life that are bleeding in silence. Expose what is toxic, and cleanse me with Your living water. Help me surrender my pain instead of reacting from it. I confess the places where I've tried to heal on my own, and I ask for Your mercy. Where there was betrayal, bring truth. Where there was sin, bring repentance. And where there was devastation, bring deliverance.

In Jesus' name, Amen.

Affirmation

Lord, I trust You to reveal the truth and guide me through this storm. I release bitterness and embrace Your peace.

Scripture

"The Lord is nigh unto them that are of a broken heart; and saveth such as be of a contrite spirit." — Psalm 34:18 (KJV)

Chapter 2

The Plague of Frogs: Chaos and Confusion

In Egypt, the second plague came like a tidal wave of chaos. Frogs filled every space, beds, kitchens, streets, and even royal chambers. They invaded what was once clean and ordered, making life feel unbearable and defiled.

That's exactly how my life felt after the truth of Dwight's affair surfaced. The plague of chaos had entered my home.

What began as a slow untangling in the previous chapter becomes a full-blown storm here. After Dwight's betrayal, the emotional floodgates broke wide open. He not only cheated, but he also flaunted it. He told mutual friends. He didn't even try to hide the other woman. It was as though he took pleasure in seeing my heart collapse under the weight of humiliation.

And yet, in that season, I was not only fighting external battles. Inside me, a second plague was spreading, the one of confusion, guilt, shame, and spiritual torment. I found myself in a tug-of-war between truth and emotion, faith and flesh. I was a minister, a mother, and a wife. But now I was also a betrayed woman, angry, tired, and tempted to abandon everything I believed.

"For where your treasure is, there your heart will be also."

—Matthew 6:21

As Dwight became colder and more manipulative, I tried to maintain a sense of normalcy for my kids, for the church, and for myself. I wore a smile in public while privately screaming in silence. He began weaponizing our children, portraying himself as the doting father while subtly undermining me. His family joined in, covering for him and fueling his denial.

The weight of it all nearly crushed me. The façade I had so carefully constructed for the public eye, the "strong Christian woman", was crumbling. I had counseled others through storms like this, pointing them to faith and perseverance. But now I was struggling to believe those same words for myself.

I wanted to believe that things could be restored. I wanted to believe that my prayers would change him. But Dwight laughed at my faith. He mocked my prayers, dismissed my prophetic dreams, and belittled my convictions.

> "For your ways are in full view of the Lord, and He examines all your paths."
>
> —*Proverbs 5:21*

I still remember how smug he looked when speaking about his mistress, as if he had the right to pursue happiness at my expense. But what hurt even more was his denial. After openly flaunting the affair, he suddenly began claiming it never happened. His gaslighting was as suffocating as the sin itself.

Like the frogs that overran Egypt, the chaos in my life touched everything. Financial instability, emotional turmoil, sleepless nights, broken trust, it never stopped. Every time I managed to clean up one area, another crisis erupted. There was no intimacy, no peace, no unity, only distance, fear, and confusion.

My children appeared stable, but I could see the subtle changes. Their routines, school, church, and activities continued, but their eyes told a different story. There was confusion, silence, and questions they didn't know how to ask. I was watching my family disintegrate while trying to keep everyone afloat.

In desperation, I turned again to my ex-boyfriend, the one I had reached out to before. I knew it was wrong. God had warned me repeatedly. But I was hungry for connection, for someone to see me, to value me, to make me feel alive again. I told myself that maybe he could help me forget the pain, even just for a while.

But deep down, I knew the truth: *I was running*. And I was running straight into more destruction.

> "No temptation has overtaken you except what is common to mankind. And God is faithful; He will not let you be tempted beyond what you can bear."
>
> —*1 Corinthians 10:13*

Despite God's repeated warnings, I kept seeing my ex. I told myself it was temporary, that I could control it. But I was lying to myself. The relationship was not healing me; it was deepening the wound. My emotions had become my master, and I was losing sight of who I was.

And during this, I didn't just lose Dwight; I was starting to lose *myself*.

I had spent years building my life around roles: wife, mother, minister. Now, with those roles opening up before my eyes, I was left with the question: *Who am I without them?*

The divorce process dragged on for two painful years. Two years of court hearings, legal delays, financial losses, and spiritual silence. I watched my income shrink, my properties fall into dispute, and my name dragged through the mud. And all the while, Dwight's heart only grew harder.

> "And Pharaoh hardened his heart this time also and did not let the people go."
> — *Exodus 8:32*

Still, through all the chaos, through all the frogs in my life, God was saying something to me. I couldn't always hear Him through the noise of my rebellion and grief, but He had not left me. He was still calling me to trust Him, to let go of the things I had tried to control, and to stop building escape routes that led to deeper bondage.

I just wasn't ready to listen… yet.

Devotional Prayer

Father,

When chaos surrounds me, You remain constant. When confusion clouds my thoughts, Your voice still speaks. Help me recognize the patterns in my life that keep repeating, those "frogs" of pain, compromise, and distraction. Lord, bring clarity to my confusion, order to my disorder, and conviction to my rebellion. Where I've allowed emotions to rule, restore Your peace. Where I've clung to people instead of You, give me the strength to let go. I choose to trust You, even when I don't understand the path. Bring beauty out of this chaos and teach me to hear You again.

In Jesus' name, Amen.

Affirmation:

I reject confusion and embrace the wisdom of God. I am not a prisoner of manipulation, but a child of the Most High.

Scripture

"For God is not the author of confusion, but of peace, as in all churches of the saints." — 1 Corinthians 14:33 (KJV)

Chapter 3

The Plague of Lice – Internal Struggles and Hidden Sins

In Egypt, the plague of lice came suddenly. Dust from the ground transformed into countless tiny creatures that invaded the people and animals, clinging to their skin and burrowing into their lives. It wasn't a loud or dramatic plague like the others, but rather a small, silent, but unrelenting one.

That is exactly how this season of my life felt.

After the chaos of the "frogs", the arguments, betrayals, and manipulations came a more personal, suffocating plague. The lice in my spirit weren't visible to the world, but I could feel them in my soul. They represented the internal struggles, the private sins, the unspoken bitterness, and the guilt I could no longer hide.

The truth was, I had been carrying these "lice" long before the marriage collapsed. My tendency to ignore God's warnings, my need to control the image of a "perfect" life, my resentment that I refused to lay at His feet, these had been there for years. Now, in the aftermath of Dwight's betrayal and my own, they had multiplied.

I had been betrayed, yes, but I had also betrayed. I had broken vows not only to Dwight but to God. I had stood at an altar before witnesses and promised to love, honor, and remain faithful. And yet, in my woundedness, I had stepped outside the marriage, rationalizing it as comfort for my pain.

The guilt was worse than the act itself. It didn't fade; it festered. It whispered accusations in the quiet. It followed me into prayer. It stood beside me when I tried to minister.

"For as he thinketh in his heart, so is he." – *Proverbs 23:7*

In my heart, I had allowed bitterness and resentment to become my constant meditation. Instead of guarding my mind with God's promises, I entertained thoughts of revenge, self-pity, and justification. The lice of sin don't begin on the outside; they start in the mind, where we allow lies to breed.

The heaviest weight of this plague was not Dwight's behavior; it was the distance I felt from my Lord.

"Your sins have hidden His face from you, so that He will not hear." – *Isaiah 59:2*

I knew He hadn't abandoned me, but I couldn't deny that my choices had built a wall between us. Prayer became hard. Worship felt empty. I stopped lingering at the altar because I could no longer lift my hands without feeling the sting of hypocrisy.

I wanted His presence, but I didn't want to fully surrender. I wanted His healing, but I didn't want the exposure that repentance would require.

Dwight, ever the charmer, knew how to twist narratives. He laughed off serious conversations, using humor as a shield for his lies. In front of the children, he played the role of the ideal father, subtly implying that I was unstable, overly emotional, or the root of the household tension.

His family enabled him. Any disagreement between us became a public tribunal where I was outnumbered. They excused his infidelity, minimized his neglect, and painted my resistance as rebellion. This left me feeling like I was living inside a fog of deception where truth was constantly rewritten.

My children were caught in the middle, though they didn't always have words for it. On the outside, their routines continued: school, activities, and church. But at home, the silence between us grew heavier. They didn't share their days the way they used to. I could see the confusion in their eyes when they heard conflicting stories from their father and me.

The lice had infested my home, not physical pests, but emotional ones. Small lies, hidden resentments, unspoken pain, spreading, multiplying, suffocating.

Even in this place, God's voice reached me.

> "Come now, and let us reason together, says the Lord: though your sins be as scarlet, they shall be as white as snow." – *Isaiah 1:18*

This was His invitation, not to minimize my sin, but to wash it away. The plague of lice was showing me that before I could see deliverance in my marriage, my ministry, or my family, I had to deal with what was within me.

Repentance was not optional; it was my only way forward.

The hardest part of this plague was realizing that I could not simply "clean up" my situation without dealing with the root issues. The lice represented my inner life, my thought patterns, my unconfessed sins, my pride. And no matter how much I tried to hide behind ministry, motherhood, or outward composure, they kept resurfacing.

I knew better. I knew God's voice. I knew the warnings He had given me long before all of this. But I had ignored them.

"Be sure your sins will find you out." – *Numbers 32:23*

This plague forced me to admit that my pain did not excuse my disobedience. Dwight's betrayal did not justify mine. My role as a victim did not cancel my role as a sinner in need of grace.

And so, I stood at a crossroads: stay in the cycle of shame and self-protection, or surrender fully to the God who could cleanse even the deepest infestations of my soul.

Before we move forward, I want to pause here and speak directly to you, the reader. This chapter isn't just about what happened in my home, it's about what might be happening in your heart right now. The "lice" in our lives are often the things no one else can see: the thoughts we entertain, the bitterness we nurture, the compromises we justify.

The questions that follow aren't here to shame you, they're here to guide you toward the healing that begins in the hidden places. Take time to sit with them, journal your answers, and let the Holy Spirit shine His light in the corners of your soul.

Devotional Prayer

Father,

You see what no one else can see, the hidden places, the unspoken thoughts, the compromises I try to bury. Today, I invite You to search me and know me. Reveal the "lice" in my spirit that I have ignored or excused. Wash me clean with the blood of Jesus, and restore my intimacy with You. Remove the walls that my sin has built, and teach me to walk in truth again. Even in my failures, remind me that Your mercy is new every morning.

In Jesus' name, Amen.

Affirmation

Lord, search my heart and cleanse me from anything that is not of You. I walk in purity and truth.

Scripture

"Create in me a clean heart, O God; and renew a right spirit within me." — Psalm 51:10 (KJV)

Chapter 4
The Plague of Flies – Swarmed by Chaos

The plague of flies descended upon Egypt in swarms, thick and inescapable. They covered the land, invaded homes, disrupted every routine, and made life unbearable. Flies aren't like other pests; they don't merely annoy, they corrupt. They contaminate everything they touch.

That's how my life felt in this season, overrun by chaos that never let up.

The plague of lice had forced me to confront the hidden sins within myself, but the plague of flies represented the outside forces that now swarmed me. I was in the thick of the divorce process, and each day felt like a battle for my sanity.

By this point, Dwight had perfected his public narrative. In his version, I was the one who abandoned the marriage, the one who "gave up," the unstable one. He left out the parts about his infidelity, his manipulation, his refusal to repent.

And the most devastating tactic? He used our children as pawns.

Their love for him became his bargaining chip. He positioned himself as the perfect father, present, attentive, and fun, while subtly undermining my role as mother. He would plant seeds of doubt in their minds, twisting my discipline into cruelty, my boundaries into bitterness. Over time, I could see those seeds taking root in ways that pierced me deeper than any insult he could throw.

"The thief comes only to steal and kill and destroy." – *John 10:10*

Dwight had stolen my peace, chipped away at my dignity, and trampled my trust. But even as I recognized it, I felt powerless to stop it. The buzzing of these "flies" of manipulation, gossip, and emotional warfare was constant and loud.

The external attacks stirred up internal storms. Anger, guilt, shame, heartbreak, they didn't come in waves anymore; they were constant, like a background noise I couldn't silence. I hated Dwight for what he had done. But in the quiet moments, I realized I hated myself more, for ignoring God's warnings, for compromising my own convictions, for staying in places I should have left long ago.

I heard the Lord's voice reminding me of what He had already spoken: I could not fight chaos with chaos. I had to surrender the battle to Him.

> "And the Lord said to Moses, 'Stretch out your hand… and the flies will swarm the land of Egypt.'" – *Exodus 8:21*

And yet, even with this clear word from God, I still made choices that kept me bound.

I continued seeing my ex-boyfriend, convincing myself it was temporary and harmless. I told myself I could handle it, that I was strong enough to control the situation. But the truth was, I was letting my emotions lead me instead of God.

> "A double-minded man is unstable in all his ways." –
> *James 1:8*

I was living that instability, torn between wanting deliverance and clinging to the very things keeping me in bondage. God had already warned me that if I pursued marriage with my ex, I would lose everything. I would enter it empty, stripped of resources, position, and peace. Yet the pull of my loneliness kept me from fully letting go.

Dwight fought just as hard, not for reconciliation, but for control. He dragged out the legal process, contested every decision, and clung to every asset not out of need, but out of spite. He didn't just want to win; he wanted to keep me bound to him emotionally and financially.

It felt like the flies were everywhere, buzzing lies into the ears of others, contaminating relationships, swarming my mind when I tried to rest, clouding my prayers.

And yet, even in the swarm, God was still speaking.

He reminded me that the flies were temporary, but my obedience to Him was eternal. He called me to see beyond the immediate chaos and into the promise of deliverance. But to get there, I would have to unclench my fists, release my need to control, and fully trust Him with the outcome.

This plague taught me that the enemy thrives in confusion, but God's deliverance begins with clarity. The flies could not be stopped by my arguments, my defenses, or my strategies, they could only be removed by the power of God.

And so I began to pray differently, not "God, fix him" or "God, prove me right," but "God, cleanse this atmosphere. Remove the swarm from my life. Teach me to stand still and see Your salvation."

I didn't feel an immediate breakthrough, but I felt a shift, a quiet knowing that if I would truly let go, God would fight for me.

Before we turn the page, I want you to pause. The "flies" in our lives can look like toxic people, constant drama, or even our own anxious thoughts. Sometimes, they are the lies the enemy whispers to make us doubt our worth.

The questions below are not just for self-examination, they're a chance to let God identify the swarms that have been distracting, tormenting, or contaminating your life. Let Him reveal what He wants to remove so you can step into the freedom He has prepared.

Devotional Prayer

Father,

I come before You weary from the swarms that have clouded my mind and disrupted my peace. Today, I surrender the chaos to You. Remove every "fly" that contaminates my thoughts, relationships, and heart. Silence the lies and replace them with Your truth. Give me the courage to let go of what keeps me bound, and the faith to trust You with the battle I cannot fight alone. Lord, clear the air around me so I can breathe freely in Your presence.

In Jesus' name, Amen.

Affirmation

I will not be overcome by chaos. God is my refuge, and I stand firm in His protection.

Scripture

"God is our refuge and strength, a very present help in trouble." — Psalm 46:1 (KJV)

Chapter 5

The Plague of Livestock – Losing What Sustained Me

When the fifth plague struck Egypt, the livestock, their wealth, provisions, and source of daily strength were destroyed. In an instant, the animals that carried burdens, tilled the fields, provided milk, and served as food were gone. Egypt's economy and identity collapsed under the weight of loss.

This was more than just a blow to their agriculture; it was a stripping of pride. They had placed confidence in what they owned, what they controlled, what they thought could never be taken. And then, in one plague, it was gone.

That is exactly what this season felt like for me. My livestock was not cattle or oxen; it was the things I believed would sustain me: my marriage, my possessions, my income, my reputation, and the illusion of stability for my children. One by one, God allowed those things to be stripped away, not to destroy me, but to reveal that He alone is the source of my strength.

The plague of livestock forced me to face the truth: Dwight and I had never built our marriage on anything real. From the start, there was no true foundation, no genuine love, no deep bond of trust, no spiritual agreement. I didn't love him, not in the way a wife should love her husband. I married him because I thought it was the right thing to do for my children, hoping that with time and prayer, feelings might grow.

But love cannot be manufactured, and survival is not a foundation.

No matter how hard I tried to create a connection, it slipped away like sand through my fingers. I prayed, fasted, and prophesied, warning Dwight that God was revealing His judgment if he didn't repent. But like Pharaoh, Dwight hardened his heart. He dismissed my warnings, mocking the very voice of God.

"But Pharaoh's heart was hard, and he would not listen, just as the Lord had said." — *Exodus 7:13*

Like Pharaoh, Dwight saw himself as untouchable. He carried himself with an air of arrogance, convinced that nothing could break him, no warning could move him, and no judgment could reach him. He believed that the life we had built, the properties, the businesses, the income, the reputation, was secured by his own strength. He mocked the idea that God could take it all away. His pride blinded him, and like Pharaoh, that pride would eventually be his downfall.

But here was the painful truth: while Dwight's pride was hardening his heart, I was starting to lose everything, too. My faith felt fragile, my hope was slipping through my fingers, and my sense of direction was clouded by constant chaos. Our marriage had never been built on a foundation of love, trust, or unity; it was built on survival. And survival can only last so long before it collapses.

We were strangers living in the same house, coexisting without connection. I kept telling myself I was staying for the sake of the children, to give them stability. But there was no stability left to give. Dwight used the children as pawns in his manipulation. He wore the mask of the perfect father, carefully crafting his image in front of them while quietly turning their hearts against me. He planted subtle lies, played the victim, and made me look like the villain.

And his manipulation didn't stop with the children; it extended to his family. They backed him at every turn, reinforcing his version of the truth and leaving me isolated. I was left to pick up the pieces alone, holding a crumbling household together with hands too weak to bear the weight.

I tried to shield my children from the chaos, but how do you protect them from a collapsing foundation? How do you explain that their father's actions were wrong without tearing down their love for him? How do you convince yourself that sacrificing your own peace is worth it just so they can have the illusion of a whole family?

It was in that place of despair that the plague of livestock became real to me. Egypt's livestock represented their wealth, their stability, their very sustenance, and in one blow, God stripped it away. My marriage was the same. It looked alive from the outside, but it was dead inside. It had been the source I leaned on, the structure I tried to build my life upon, but it was hollow. It was never grounded in love or obedience to God. And just like the plague, everything I relied on for stability began to die before my eyes.

"The Lord gave, and the Lord has taken away; blessed be the name of the Lord." — *Job 1:21*

I cried out to God, asking why He was letting it all fall apart. Why strip me of the very things I thought were holding me together? But deep down, I knew the answer: He was teaching me to rely on Him alone. He was stripping away every false foundation so I could learn that my security was never meant to come from Dwight, from possessions, or from status; it was meant to come from the Lord alone.

Like the Israelites wandering in the wilderness, I was terrified of the unknown. The wilderness felt like a place of emptiness, but God was showing me it was a place of dependence. He wanted me to trust Him in the absence of provision, to see that He was my true Provider.

The marriage became a battle I could no longer fight. Eventually, I stopped. I stopped trying to fix what was unfixable, to resuscitate what God had already declared dead.

When Dwight's affair came to light, it felt like the final blow, the last plague that confirmed what I already knew in my spirit. He bragged about it at first, flaunting his betrayal as though I was supposed to accept it. To make it worse, the woman was someone I knew, which cut me even deeper. But when Dwight realized I was ready to leave, ready to walk away for good, suddenly he shifted. He began denying the affair, rewriting the narrative, trying to convince me I had imagined the whole thing.

But it was too late. I had seen the truth with my own eyes. I had carried the weight of his betrayal in my soul. His denial couldn't erase the scars or undo the devastation. I was ready, finally, for divorce. Ready to stop clinging to brokenness. Ready to let go.

Yet even then, I was not innocent. His disrespect cut deeply, but so did my own compromises. My heart, heavy with bitterness, had driven me into sin.

"Do not be unequally yoked together with unbelievers. For what fellowship has righteousness with lawlessness? And what communion has light with darkness?" — *2 Corinthians 6:14*

I didn't just lose trust in Dwight, I lost trust in myself. I allowed pain and anger to lead me into the arms of my ex-boyfriend, desperate for comfort and connection. But even in that, God had already warned me. Through dreams, visions, and prayer, He told me this relationship would not last, that I was walking straight into another disaster. I ignored His voice, convincing myself it would be different this time. But deep in my spirit, I knew the truth: I was building another house without God, and unless He built it, it was destined to fall.

"Unless the Lord builds the house, the builders labor in vain." — *Psalm 127:1*

I wanted so badly to fill the emptiness Dwight left behind that I ran to a counterfeit. I needed to learn to let God fill the void, not another man.

And the losses kept coming. God was stripping me bare, not to destroy me, but to rebuild me. One by one, the things I leaned on were taken: properties lost, income decreased, children pulled from private schools. I watched my life unravel piece by piece, but I also began to understand: this wasn't just about losing Dwight. It was about losing everything that had falsely sustained me so I could finally learn to be sustained by God alone.

This chapter of my life was more than the death of a marriage, it was the death of survival mode. It was the breaking of a false foundation, so God could lay a new one in His strength.

I had to let the old things die so that God could bring something new to life.

This plague isn't just about what I lost; it's about what you may be losing, too. Sometimes God allows our "livestock" to die, the resources, relationships, or structures we thought would carry us, because He wants us to rely only on Him. Take time now to ask Him: what am I clinging to that You are asking me to release?

Devotional Prayer

Father,

You are my provider, my strength, and my source. Forgive me for leaning on things that could never sustain me. Teach me to see loss not as punishment, but as preparation. Strip away what is false so that only what is eternal remains. Help me to release the old and trust You to bring forth the new. Even when I feel empty, remind me that in You, I will never lack.

In Jesus' name, Amen.

Affirmation

My security is not in material things but in the Lord. He is my provider, and He restores all that I have lost.

Scripture

"But my God shall supply all your need according to his riches in glory by Christ Jesus." — Philippians 4:19 (KJV)

Chapter 6
The Plague of Boils – Pain That Won't Heal

In Egypt, when the plague of boils struck, it left visible sores on the skin of every man and beast. The pain was not hidden; it was raw, exposed, and undeniable. It was a judgment that could not be ignored or explained away.

That is how I felt at this stage of my journey. My life bore the visible scars of betrayal and brokenness. The wounds of my marriage were not just internal anymore; they showed up in my speech, my emotions, my children, my finances, and even in my ministry. I was marked by pain that refused to heal, by wounds that burned long after the initial blow.

The plague of boils was not just physical; it was emotional, spiritual, and mental torment. And like Egypt, I found myself sitting in suffering I could not escape.

By now, Dwight's heart was so hardened that it reminded me daily of Pharaoh. God had sent warning after warning, through my dreams, through prophecy, through the counsel of others, but Dwight mocked every word.

"But the Lord hardened Pharaoh's heart and he would not listen." – *Exodus 9:12*

He laughed at the idea that his actions carried consequences. He brushed off my pleas for repentance as emotional outbursts, not words from the Lord. His arrogance grew bolder even after the affair came to light. First, he bragged about it, then he denied it when divorce papers were filed, trying to rewrite history as if the truth could be erased.

But no matter what he said, the scars he left on me remained. The affair was only one boil on the surface of a much deeper sickness. The real affliction was his manipulation, his emotional abuse, and his relentless ability to twist every narrative so I was painted as the villain.

Dwight was cunning in how he used words, especially with the children. He knew how to position himself as the victim, planting seeds like: "Your mom is trying to *tear this* family *apart.*" With each word, he poisoned their trust in me and fed their pity for him.

"For the mouth speaks what the heart is full of." – *Luke 6:45*

His heart was full of bitterness and pride, and his words became daggers. To those who didn't know the truth, he looked like a devoted father and wounded husband. To me, he was a man weaponizing lies to maintain control.

The silence that fell over my home was suffocating. The children, caught between competing stories, withdrew into themselves. Conversations became strained. The heaviness was so thick it felt like the air itself was infected.

Even as I moved toward freedom, the boils of emotional pain continued to sting. Every conversation turned into an argument. Every phone call about the children became a battlefield. Every attempt to stand my ground was met with new accusations and fresh wounds.

I wanted to heal, but the pain was relentless. It followed me into prayer, into church, into sleepless nights. It was not just Dwight's actions that wounded me; it was my own guilt and shame for the choices I had made along the way.

And then there was my ex, the man I thought might be my escape. For a time, he made me feel seen after years of being invisible. He gave me the illusion of comfort, the hope of starting over. But God's voice pierced through the illusion: "This is not the answer. This marriage will not last."

I didn't want to believe it. I wanted the pain to end quickly, to cover my wounds with a new relationship. But God was asking me to sit in my pain, to face it, and to let Him heal it instead of running to temporary relief.

Dwight pushed every button he could, trying to keep me bound in anger, fear, and dependency. He threatened me with financial ruin, telling me that leaving him meant I would leave with nothing. And in many ways, he was right. I was leaving behind houses, income, and the life I thought I needed.

But maybe leaving with nothing was exactly what I needed.

Because when I had nothing left, I would finally realize that Jesus was all I truly had, and all I truly needed.

"He heals the brokenhearted and binds up their wounds." – *Psalm 147:3*

The boils on my soul did not disappear overnight. Some left scars I will carry for the rest of my life. But those scars became testimonies. They whispered not only of the pain I endured, but of the strength God gave me to survive. They reminded me that I had been through hell and still stood on holy ground.

I realized something profound in this season: healing does not come by holding on to anger or searching for love in broken places. Healing comes only by surrender, by laying the wounds bare before the Lord and letting Him touch what no man can heal.

Dwight's heart remained hard, but mine could not afford to. If I kept my heart hardened too, I would become just like him, bitter, prideful, blind to the truth.

The plagues were never meant to destroy me. They were meant to free me. And freedom, I was learning, does not come without pain.

The plague of boils shows us that wounds must be faced, not covered. Pain unacknowledged becomes infection. As you reflect, ask yourself: where are the "boils" in your life, wounds that refuse to heal because you've been avoiding them, covering them, or trying to fix them in your own strength? God wants to touch those places and bind them up with His love.

Closing Devotional Prayer

Father,

You see the wounds I try to hide. You know the pain that lingers like boils on my soul, the scars that remind me of betrayal and loss. Today, I lay them at Your feet. Heal me where no one else can. Bind up my broken heart and make me whole again. Teach me not to cover my wounds with counterfeit comfort, but to trust You to heal me completely. May my scars become testimonies of Your power to redeem.

In Jesus' name, Amen.

Affirmation

I declare healing over my body, mind, and soul. Pain will not define me; God's restoration is upon me.

Scripture

"He healeth the broken in heart, and bindeth up their wounds." — Psalm 147:3 (KJV)

Chapter 7
The Plague of Hail – Shattered Dreams

When the plague of hail fell upon Egypt, it struck with a fury no one could escape. The storm came with thunder and fire, ice rained down from heaven, and every crop, every tree, every plant was destroyed. What had once been alive and flourishing was shattered in a single season. That storm didn't just damage, it devastated.

That was how my life felt for the next two years. Everything I had built, everything I had dreamed, every piece of stability I thought I could lean on, it was all broken by storm after storm. Each day felt like another piece of hail crashing down on my head, leaving me bruised, weary, and wondering if there would be anything left of me when it was all over.

By the time the divorce began, Dwight and I were no longer living together. We had already separated, and whatever bond we once shared had been severed. I thought leaving Dwight would bring relief, that the decision to divorce and live apart would free me from the storm. But instead, the storm grew worse.

What I thought might take a few months dragged into two long years. The court battles seemed endless. Hearing after hearing, motion after motion, it felt like the system itself was being used as a weapon against me. Every day was filled with paperwork, legal fees, and the crushing weight of uncertainty.

Dwight refused to cooperate. He would not negotiate, he would not sign off on refinancing, and he would not agree to sell any properties. His stubbornness left millions of dollars at risk, but he didn't care. It was as if he wanted me to lose everything, even if it meant he lost everything too.

The longer the fight continued, the more indifferent he became. I saw his heart grow harder, just like Pharaoh's when Moses warned him of God's judgment. And as his heart hardened, mine began to as well. I grew tired, cold, and numb. It was my way of protecting myself from the pain of watching everything I had worked so hard for fall apart.

The truth was, Dwight had no idea how much was at stake. I had been the one who studied real estate, who learned, put in the money, and sacrificed to build what we had. He had simply benefited from my hard work. But when the marriage crumbled, he acted as if everything we had built was his to control.

He thought by stalling, by dragging things out, he was stopping me. What he didn't realize was that his refusal to act wasn't stopping me; it was only destroying the very foundation he stood on. He was setting himself up for failure, and in the process, putting the future of our children at risk.

Property after property slipped through my fingers. One by one, the houses, the land, the accounts were taken from me, sold off, or lost to debt. I had built those things with the hope that they would create a safe haven for my family, especially for my children. But the storm didn't spare even that. The home I dreamed would be our refuge, the place where my children could always feel safe, but it was gone.

The loss wasn't just financial. It was emotional. It was spiritual. I felt like every piece of stability I had given my children was stripped away.

My children were used to a certain life. They had grown up in private schools, shielded from the kind of struggles I had known as a child. I wanted them to have opportunities I never had. But as the storm raged, I couldn't keep up with the tuition payments.

The day I realized I couldn't pay for their schools anymore broke me. I tried to shield them from the full weight of what was happening, but children always see more than we think. I saw the confusion in their eyes, the sadness they tried to hide, the way they didn't talk as freely as they once did.

Their world was crumbling alongside mine, and I felt helpless. As a mother, I wanted to cover them from the hail, but it was striking all of us.

As if the financial and emotional storms weren't enough, Dwight's manipulation continued. He used the children as pawns, twisting the story to make himself look like the victim and me like the villain.

To others, he painted a picture of himself as the faithful father, the one who wanted to save the family, while I was the one tearing it apart. He ignored the cracks he had caused long before the divorce. He erased the truth of his betrayal and replaced it with lies.

Even as everything fell apart, he refused to admit his role in the destruction.

"But Pharaoh's heart was hardened, and he would not let the Israelites go." – *Exodus 9:35*

Like Pharaoh, no matter how much destruction the storm caused, he would not let go.

In the middle of all this, I clung to something I thought would protect me, but it was only another storm in disguise, my ex-boyfriend.

He became my escape, my moment of comfort when everything around me felt unbearable. He made me feel wanted and loved in ways Dwight never had. For a time, it felt like he was the shelter I needed.

But God's voice was clear in my Spirit: *"If you marry him, it will not last. You will enter the marriage with nothing."*

Still, I tried to silence the warnings. I convinced myself that this was different, that he could be the one to finally cherish me. But the deeper I went into the relationship, the louder God's voice became.

"Unless the Lord builds the house, the builders labor in vain." – *Psalm 127:1*

I was trying to build something new while standing on the ruins of my old life. I hadn't given God time to heal me, to rebuild me, to lay a fresh foundation. Instead, I was carrying my wounds into something new, hoping a man could fill a void only God could fill.

Rather than finding healing, I found more confusion.

As the battles continued, I felt the weight of loss in every area of my life.

Legal fees piled high. Bills went unpaid. My income was drained. My children's lives were disrupted. My dreams of creating a legacy for them slipped away. And through it all, Dwight used every delay, every obstacle, every loophole to remind me that I was losing everything.

The financial strain was suffocating. It felt like no matter how hard I worked, I was drowning under the pressure. The harder I tried to hold on, the more it slipped through my fingers.

There were nights I cried out to God, asking Him why He was letting this storm rage against me. Why did everything I touch seem to break? Why did my children have to suffer for choices they did not make?

And then I remembered His Word:

"I have indeed seen the misery of my people… I have heard them crying out… and I am concerned about their suffering."
– *Exodus 3:7*

God reminded me that He saw me, He heard me, and He was concerned about me, even when I felt invisible, even when my prayers felt weak. He was not absent from the storm.

The hailstorm was breaking me, yes, but it was also stripping away everything that could not last. My marriage, my financial empire, my carefully built plans, all of it was being shattered so that God could rebuild me on something stronger.

I began to see that this was not punishment. It was preparation. God was not trying to destroy me; He was trying to deliver me. And freedom often comes at a cost.

Devotional Prayer

Father,

The hailstorms of life come fast and hard, and they leave behind shattered dreams and broken hearts. I confess that I have tried to find shelter in people and things that cannot truly protect me. But today, I choose to trust You as my refuge. Even in the storm, I believe You see me, You hear me, and You are preparing me for freedom. Strip away everything in my life that is not built on You, and help me stand firm on Your promises. Let my scars become a testimony of Your power to rebuild.

In Jesus' name, Amen.

Affirmation

What was meant for my harm, God will turn for my good. My dreams are being restored in His perfect time.

Scripture

"And we know that all things work together for good to them that love God, to them who are the called according to his purpose." — Romans 8:28 (KJV)

Chapter 8

The Plague of Locusts – Devouring What Remained

When the plague of locusts descended upon Egypt, it didn't leave a single green thing behind. It swept over the land like a living shadow, devouring every plant, every tree, and every hope of recovery. It was relentless. It was final.

That's how my life felt during this season, devoured piece by piece, stripped of everything I thought I had left. Just when I believed the worst was over, another wave came, eating away at what little security remained.

At that time, I was 43 years old, a Black woman raising four children, standing in the aftermath of a marriage that had been battered and broken. Two years of divorce hearings, property disputes, and endless court appearances had taken nearly everything from me.

The real estate portfolio I had built was gone. The savings account I had sacrificed to fill had been drained by legal fees and bills. My children, who once thrived in private schools, were adjusting to public classrooms and a very different life.

I felt the weight of all of it on my back, the bills stacked higher than my courage, the pressure of being both mother and father, the exhaustion of trying to hold everything together while my world collapsed around me.

I wasn't just praying anymore. I was begging. Begging God to leave me at least one thing I could hold onto.

One memory stands out even now. It may sound small to someone else, but to me it was everything. My Escalade truck.

That vehicle wasn't just a car. It was my lifeline. It got my kids to school. It allowed me to work. It gave me the sense, however small, that I still had a piece of my old life intact. When so much had already been taken, that truck became my last little sanctuary.

I remember kneeling and crying out to God: "Please, Lord. Not this. Please don't let this be taken too."

"I will restore to you the years that the swarming locust has eaten." — *Joel 2:25*

I clung to that verse. I said it over and over again, like a child rocking herself to sleep after a nightmare. Even as the locusts in my life devoured one thing after another, I believed God could restore what was lost.

But God wasn't done speaking. As I cried out for help, He reminded me of a warning He had given me before: *"If you marry your ex-boyfriend, you will enter the marriage with nothing."*

It was hard to hear it again. My ex still held a piece of my heart. In my pain, the idea of finally being with him felt like a rescue, a comfort, a way out of the nightmare Dwight had left me in.

But God's voice was clear. This wasn't just about money or property. It was about the spiritual and emotional cost. If I went down that road, I wouldn't just lose material things, I would lose myself.

"Unless the Lord builds the house, the builders labor in vain." — *Psalm 127:1*

I had built my marriage with Dwight on a foundation that could not last. Now God was warning me not to build another life on the shaky ground of loneliness and desperation.

But trusting God wasn't easy when I felt so abandoned. My prayers felt like they were bouncing off the ceiling. My dreams for my children, my hopes for my own future, they all lay in ruins.

I remember lying awake at night, staring at the ceiling, wondering how I would ever start over at 43 with four children and almost nothing to my name. The thought of it terrified me.

It wasn't just Dwight's betrayal that had left me broken. It was my own decisions too. My refusal to fully surrender. My desperate attempts to fix what only God could fix. Yet even in my rebellion, God's mercy had not left me. He was still speaking, still guiding, still offering me a way out if I was willing to take it.

Dwight, like Pharaoh, remained unrepentant. His heart was as hard as ever, refusing to take responsibility for the destruction he had caused. He mocked my faith, dismissed my prayers, and acted as though nothing was his fault.

"Do not be afraid. Stand firm and you will see the deliverance the Lord will bring you today." — *Exodus 14:13*

Those words became my anchor. I had to believe that the locusts wouldn't have the final say, that God would restore what had been devoured, even if it didn't look the way I expected.

The emotional toll was staggering. Some mornings, I would wake up and feel as though my chest was caving in from the pressure. Bills. Lawyers. Court dates. Four children who still needed their mother to show up, even when she felt like disappearing.

I tried to hide my breakdowns from them. I would cry in the shower, pray in the car, whisper to God under my breath while cooking dinner. "Please, God. Please don't let this destroy me."

The strain of being everything for everyone nearly crushed me. But every time I thought I would break completely, God carried me one more step.

What I didn't understand then was that the locusts weren't just devouring my money or my property. They were devouring my identity, the false one I had built on success, on status, on relationships that were never meant to last.

God was stripping me down to the bare wood, peeling away every layer I had used to cover my wounds. It was painful, humiliating, and frightening. Yet it was also necessary.

Sometimes God allows what we cling to to be taken away, not to punish us, but to heal us.

As the locust season dragged on, God began to show me something new: survival wasn't His plan for me. Freedom was.

Freedom from Dwight's manipulation.

Freedom from my ex-boyfriend's pull.

Freedom from my own need to control the outcome.

Freedom from defining myself by what I had or didn't have.

The locusts had stripped me bare, but they hadn't destroyed me. And maybe that's what I needed, to be stripped of everything I thought I needed so God could give me what I truly needed: Himself.

"I have indeed seen the misery of my people... I have heard them crying out... and I am concerned about their suffering."
— *Exodus 3:7*

That verse became my lifeline. God saw me. God heard me. God was concerned about me. He hadn't left me, even when it felt like He had.

Slowly, almost imperceptibly, my heart began to change. The anger started to soften. The desperation began to loosen. I started to see that the storm wasn't about Dwight or my ex-boyfriend; it was about God and me.

I had been begging God to change everything outside of me. What He wanted was to change everything inside of me.

He wanted my surrender. My trust. My heart.

And as I started to give it to Him, little by little, I began to feel a strength that wasn't my own.

Devotional Prayer

Father,

The locusts in life come to devour, to strip away, and to destroy. Yet even in the devastation, You are there. You see, You hear, and You restore. Forgive me for clinging to things and people instead of clinging to You. Help me to trust You when everything else is gone. Remind me that what I lose in the flesh, You can restore in the Spirit. Teach me to build on Your foundation alone.

In Jesus' name, Amen.

Affirmation

The enemy may have taken much, but God is the God of restoration. I will recover all.

Scripture

"And I will restore to you the years that the locust hath eaten, the cankerworm, and the caterpillar, and the palmerworm, my great army which I sent among you." — Joel 2:25 (KJV)

Chapter 9

The Plague of Darkness – Lost in the Shadows

When the plague of darkness fell on Egypt, it wasn't just the absence of sunlight. It was a heavy, suffocating blackness that pressed against the skin and filled every corner of the land for three days. People couldn't see one another. They couldn't move freely. They were paralyzed in fear.

That's how my life felt in this season, dark, thick, and suffocating. The light had gone out. The path ahead was hidden. And even though I prayed, it felt like my words disappeared into the night without an answer.

By the time the darkness set in, the locusts had already devoured what was left of my life. The houses were gone. The properties had slipped through my fingers. The savings account was empty. The stability I had worked so hard to create for my children had vanished.

Even my identity as a confident businesswoman had crumbled. I had been "the strong one," the investor, the builder. Now I was a single mother with four children, staring at unpaid bills and facing a future I couldn't see.

Matthew 6:19–21 (KJV):

"Lay not up for yourselves treasures upon earth, where moth and rust doth corrupt, and where thieves break through and steal:

But lay up for yourselves treasures in heaven, where neither moth nor rust doth corrupt, and where thieves do not break through nor steal:

For where your treasure is, there will your heart be also."

Yes, God had spared my Escalade truck, and I was thankful. But keeping my car wasn't enough to ease the fear of starting over. It was like having a candle in the middle of a blacked-out city. Helpful, but not nearly enough to light the way.

Starting over meant facing the unknown. And the unknown terrified me.

How was I supposed to rebuild my life with so little? How could I raise four children, put food on the table, and hold myself together when everything inside me felt shattered?

I had been stripped down to nothing, financially, emotionally, spiritually. My strength had limits. And as much as I tried to act brave for my children, inside I was trembling.

"Trust in the Lord with all your heart and lean not on your own understanding." — *Proverbs 3:5*

I knew this verse. I had quoted it to others. I had built my life on it in the past. But now, in the darkness, it felt like a dare. Trust Him? With *everything*? When I had so little left?

Instead of leaning fully on God, I leaned on my ex-boyfriend. I wanted to feel loved. I wanted to feel wanted. I wanted to feel safe.

Deep down, I knew God was saying, "This will not last." He had warned me before. He was warning me again. But I didn't want to hear it.

I convinced myself that my ex could give me the stability Dwight had taken from me. That he could fill the void, hold me up, and make me whole. I told myself it was harmless, that it was "just comfort" during a hard season.

But it wasn't harmless.

It was a compromise.

And compromise always costs something.

Meanwhile, Dwight's heart stayed hard, just like Pharaoh's. He still refused to take responsibility for the chaos he had caused. He still mocked my faith and dismissed my prayers. He still acted as though none of it was his fault.

And yet, even after all he had done, the idea of letting go of everything we had built together felt devastating. It's strange how the human heart clings to what is familiar, even when it's destructive.

"Do not be unequally yoked with unbelievers." — *2 Corinthians 6:14*

I had read that verse a thousand times. I had quoted it to others. Now it was staring me in the face like a mirror.

The darkness wasn't just around me. It was in me.

I was walking blindly, knowing God's voice but choosing to ignore it. I wanted to believe I could have both God's blessings and my ex-boyfriend's love, but deep down, I knew I couldn't.

Every time I prayed, I still had one foot in the past. I was clinging to a broken life while asking God to give me a new one. No wonder I felt stuck.

The darkness was suffocating because I had let it in. Fear, desperation, doubt, all of it clouded my vision and made it impossible to see what God was trying to do.

I had been so focused on what I had lost physically, houses, income, stability, that I didn't notice what I was losing spiritually. My peace was slipping away. My connection to God was weakening. My heart was hardening, not just Dwight's.

"The Lord is close to the brokenhearted and saves those who are crushed in spirit." — *Psalm 34:18*

Even in the darkness, God was still close. Even in my disobedience, He was still reaching for me.

I began to realize that I couldn't outrun the darkness. I couldn't distract myself from it. I had to face it.

Facing it meant admitting the truth:

- Dwight wasn't going to change.
- My ex-boyfriend wasn't my savior.
- My finances weren't coming back overnight.
- My old life wasn't coming back at all.

Facing the darkness meant surrender, letting God into the places I was most afraid to show Him.

And slowly, His light began to pierce the shadows. Not all at once. Not dramatically. But gently, steadily, like dawn breaking over a field.

I had to make a choice: to keep clinging to what I thought would save me or to surrender and let God truly deliver me.

It wasn't an easy choice. It didn't happen in a single moment. But step by step, prayer by prayer, I began to loosen my grip on my ex-boyfriend. I began to stop looking back at Dwight. I began to shift my eyes upward instead of outward.

The fear of losing everything didn't vanish overnight. But something inside me was shifting. I began to see that what I feared losing wasn't what God wanted for me in the first place.

Darkness can be terrifying. But sometimes darkness is the place where God does His deepest work. Seeds grow in the dark. Babies develop in the dark. Healing begins in the dark.

Maybe that's why God allowed the darkness in my life. Not to punish me, but to transform me. Not to destroy me, but to deliver me.

Dwight's hard heart mirrored Pharaoh's, but my story didn't have to end in bondage. God was still writing my Exodus.

Slowly, I began to see glimmers of hope. A check would come in just when I needed it. A friend would call at the right time. A verse would stand out during my morning reading and feel like God Himself whispering to me.

Little by little, light began to break through. It didn't remove the struggle, but it reminded me I wasn't alone.

"Even the darkness will not be dark to you; the night will shine like the day, for darkness is as light to you." — *Psalm 139:12*

God had not abandoned me. He was right there, guiding me through the shadows.

Devotional Prayer

Father,

When darkness surrounds me, help me to remember that You are still there. Even when I cannot see the way ahead, Your light never goes out. Forgive me for leaning on people instead of leaning fully on You. Teach me to trust You with every part of my life. Bring Your light into every hidden place of my heart and lead me out of the shadows into Your freedom.

In Jesus' name, Amen.

Affirmation

Even in my darkest hour, God is my light. I will not be overcome by despair, for my Redeemer lives.

Scripture

"The light shineth in darkness; and the darkness comprehended it not." — John 1:5 (KJV)

Chapter 10
The Plague of the Death of the Firstborn – Dying to Myself

The last plague that fell on Egypt was the most devastating of all. In one night, every firstborn was gone. It was a loss so deep and so final that even Pharaoh's pride could not stand against it. It broke the nation. It broke Pharaoh. It broke everything that had stood in defiance of God.

That's how my divorce felt. It wasn't just a legal ending; it was a death. It was the death of a marriage, yes, but also the death of dreams, expectations, and the life I thought I had built. Like Egypt, I had been warned. Like Pharaoh, I had held on for too long. And in the end, something had to die.

When I first married Dwight, I believed we were building something that would last forever. We had homes, businesses, and plans. We had the image of stability. But the foundation was weak, and Dwight's infidelity revealed how fragile it all was.

At first, I tried to hold it together. I prayed harder. I gave more. I tried to be more understanding. Yet, even as I begged

God to save the marriage, something inside me was also breaking. And in my pain, I made my own mistakes. I sought comfort in another man's arms, thinking it would heal me. It didn't. It only deepened my wounds.

What started as hurt grew into bitterness. And bitterness, left unchecked, turned into resentment, against Dwight, against my situation, and even against myself.

The two years waiting for the divorce to be finalized felt like wandering through the wilderness. Each day revealed anger, regret, guilt, shame, and fear. Like the Israelites after leaving Egypt, I was stripped of everything familiar.

During that time, I saw the plagues divorce can bring. Not physical plagues, but emotional and spiritual ones: hardened hearts, jealousy, unforgiveness, financial ruin, and broken trust. Divorce doesn't just end a marriage. It shakes every corner of your identity. It leaves you empty, gasping for something to fill the void.

But in the empty places, God started speaking. He showed me how tightly I had been clinging to earthly treasures, houses, status, a certain image of success, and how loosely I had been holding onto Him.

"Do not store up for yourselves treasures on earth, where moths and vermin destroy, and where thieves break in and steal. But store up for yourselves treasures in heaven. — *Matthew 6:19–20*

In the divorce, I lost more than a husband. I lost my sense of identity. I had defined myself as a wife, a homeowner, a leader in ministry, a woman others could look up to for strength and guidance. When all of that was stripped away, I was forced to face a painful question: *Who was I without the titles, the image, or the position?*

But God was using that season of breaking to show me that my worth was never in my roles or reputation. My worth was in Him alone.

As Dwight's heart hardened, mocking my faith, dismissing my warnings, and acting as though nothing could touch him, I began to see my own heart more clearly. I had been just as stubborn, trying to build a life without fully surrendering it to God.

"Whoever finds their life will lose it, and whoever loses their life for my sake will find it." — *Matthew 10:39 (NIV)*

I realized I couldn't keep clinging to my old life while asking God for a new one. Something had to die.

Letting go wasn't a one-time act, it was a daily surrender. I had to let my marriage die. I had to let my pride die, the pride that told me I had to keep it all together, that I had to protect my image, that I had to hold on to my ministerial title even when my soul was breaking.

Most of all, I had to die to myself, to my need for control, to my fear of being seen as weak, and to the belief that my value was in what I could do rather than who I was in Christ.

That meant laying down my anger, my need for control, and my desire for revenge. It meant forgiving Dwight even when he didn't deserve it. It meant forgiving myself for my own failures and sins.

"What good will it be for someone to gain the whole world, yet forfeit their soul?" — *Matthew 16:26*

As painful as it was, dying to myself brought a freedom I had never known. I no longer had to carry the burden of making everything right. I no longer had to strive to prove my worth or hold onto what was slipping away.

I could finally lay it all at the feet of Jesus, my pain, my dreams, my children, my finances, and trust Him to rebuild me in His way, in His time.

"Behold, I am doing a new thing; now it springs forth, do you not perceive it?" — *Isaiah 43:19*

That verse became a lifeline. It reminded me that even in the death of everything I had built, God was already preparing something new.

I had always thought restoration meant God would give me back what I lost: houses, income, relationships. But I began to see that God's restoration was different. It wasn't about returning to what was. It was about being made whole.

Dwight's heart never softened. His pride remained. But mine did. My heart became softer, humbler, and more willing to trust God with every part of my life. I began to see that the real treasure wasn't what I had lost but what I was gaining: a deeper walk with God, a clearer sense of purpose, and a freedom no court or man could take away.

That's when I realized this wasn't the end of a chapter, it was the beginning of something new. The victory wasn't in what I could keep or lose. The victory was in knowing my life had never been about material things.

My treasure wasn't in houses, money, or possessions. My treasure was in the Lord, and nothing, not Dwight, not the courts, not my own mistakes, could take that away from me.

At that moment, I let go. Not in defeat, but in triumph. My worth wasn't tied to what I owned or who I was married to. My worth was rooted in Christ. That was a victory no one could take from me.

Death is final, but it's also a beginning. Just as the Israelites left Egypt after the final plague, stepping into their journey of freedom, I stepped into mine.

The death of my marriage and the loss of my old life marked the end of bondage and the start of deliverance. I was no longer defined by Dwight's choices, my failures, or my losses. I was defined by God's grace.

Slowly, I began to rebuild, not with the same bricks, but with a new foundation. Prayer by prayer. Step by step. My life no longer belonged to my past. It belonged to God.

Devotional Prayer

Father,

Thank You for showing me that death is not the end, but the doorway to new life in You. Help me to die to my pride, my fears, and my need for control so that I can live fully surrendered to You. Teach me to let go of the things that are passing away and hold fast to what is eternal. Even in loss, help me to trust that You are working all things for my good.

In Jesus' name, Amen.

Affirmation

I surrender all to the Lord. Through Him, I am renewed, and my new season is here.

Scripture

"Therefore if any man be in Christ, he is a new creature: old things are passed away; behold, all things are become new." — 2 Corinthians 5:17 (KJV)

Conclusion
From Plague to Purpose

When I look back now, I can see it so clearly. What I thought was destruction was actually deliverance. What I believed was punishment was really preparation. Each loss, each betrayal, each painful chapter of my life was God's way of loosening my grip on what was temporary so that I could embrace what was eternal.

For years, I thought my identity was rooted in my marriage, my finances, and the things I had built. I thought my worth was in being a wife, a provider, a mother who could hold everything together. But divorce, like the plagues of Egypt, stripped me of every illusion and showed me the truth. My identity was never in Dwight. It was never in properties, bank accounts, or cars. My identity was in Christ, and no plague, no divorce, no betrayal could take that away.

"And we know that in all things God works for the good of those who love Him, who have been called according to His purpose. — *Romans 8:28 (NIV)*

It has been twenty years since I walked through that fire. Time has a way of softening pain but sharpening perspective.

Looking back, I can see God's hand in every detail, the timing, the losses, even the moments when I thought He was silent.

What the enemy meant for harm, God used for good. I lost material things, but I gained wisdom. I lost a marriage, but I found my true purpose. I was stripped of what was temporary so I could embrace what was eternal.

Back then, I thought I was being undone. Today, I know I was being remade.

Like the Israelites leaving Egypt after the final plague, I emerged from my divorce not just as a survivor, but as someone set free. The plagues of my life were not random punishments. They were steps in a journey toward freedom.

I had walked through my own version of every plague:

- Frogs of chaos filling every corner of my life.
- Lice of hidden sins that burrowed deep inside me.
- Flies of manipulation swarming around my family.
- Livestock lost, my stability stripped away.
- Boils of pain that refused to heal.
- Hail of shattered dreams raining down on every plan.

- Locusts devouring what little remained.

- Darkness closing in when I could no longer see my way forward.

- And finally, the death of the firstborn, the death of my old self.

But each plague was also an invitation: an invitation to trust God, to let go, to surrender, and to find my true identity in Him.

Because of that painful season, I am now walking in the fullness of my calling. I have rebuilt my life, not on shifting sand, but on the solid rock of Christ. My prayer life is stronger. My faith is deeper. My joy is real, not dependent on circumstances.

I have seen God restore, heal, and elevate me beyond anything I could have imagined back then. The plague of divorce did not define me; it refined me. It burned away the parts of me that were never meant to last and revealed the gold of His purpose in my life.

"The Lord is my rock, my fortress and my deliverer; my God is my rock, in whom I take refuge." —*Psalm 18:2*

This book is not just a story of survival. It's a symbol of victory. It's a roadmap for anyone walking through their own plagues, whether it's divorce, betrayal, financial loss, or a personal crisis of faith.

If God could do it for me, He can do it for you. You are not alone. The same God who parted the Red Sea, who brought water from a rock, who led His people by a pillar of fire, is the same God who will lead you out of your Egypt and into your promised land.

You may be stripped bare right now. You may feel like the locusts have devoured everything, like darkness has swallowed your hope, like death has taken your dreams. But know this: God is not done. His purpose for you is not over. The plagues are not your ending; they are your passageway.

The shift for me came when I realized that freedom is not just surviving the plagues, it's stepping into the calling God has for you on the other side. My calling became clearer once I stopped clinging to what I had lost and started embracing what God was trying to give me.

Today, I walk in my calling as a minister, a prophetess, and a woman who understands both loss and restoration. I speak not from theory but from experience. I mentor, I teach, and I testify to God's goodness because I have lived it. The testimony of my life is proof that no matter how deep the pit, God's arm is long enough to pull you out.

If you are reading this and you feel trapped in your own Egypt, remember: God's deliverance may not look the way you expect, but it will always be enough. His timing may feel slow, but it is perfect. His stripping away may feel cruel, but it is merciful. He removes only what cannot sustain you so that He can give you what will.

"He has made everything beautiful in its time." — *Ecclesiastes 3:11*

Do not let the pain of your plagues convince you that God has abandoned you. He is with you in every loss, every heartbreak, and every night of darkness. He is not trying to destroy you; He is trying to deliver you.

About the Author

Prophetess Catherine Matthews is a divinely anointed minister, seasoned author, and passionate speaker with decades of experience in ministry, business, and mentorship. Called by God to share His message of healing, deliverance, and prophetic truth, she has dedicated her life to uplifting others through the Word of God and the power of the Holy Spirit.

In her transformative book, A Plague of a Divorce, she explores the deep emotional and spiritual struggles of relationships and divorce, drawing a powerful parallel between the ten plagues of Egypt and the trials couples face when their covenant begins to unravel. This book, birthed through divine revelation, became not only a message for others but also a prophetic warning to her own life, as God spoke through its pages.

Ordained many years ago, she faithfully answered God's call as part of the fivefold ministry, walking in the prophetic office described in Isaiah 61:1 (KJV) — "The Spirit of the Lord GOD is upon me; because the LORD hath anointed me to preach good tidings unto the meek; he hath sent me to bind up the brokenhearted, to proclaim liberty to the captives, and the opening of the prison to them that are bound."

Throughout her life, Prophetess Catherine has witnessed countless miracles, including the Lord's miraculous, supernatural healing of her body, enabling her to bear four beautiful children whom she dedicated back to God. Today, those children are grown and walking in their divine purpose.

Out of love and devotion to family, she set aside active ministry for a season to care for her mother until her passing, embracing this responsibility as a God-ordained priority (1 Timothy 5:8 KJV). This period became a time of preparation and refinement for her future ministry, demonstrating that obedience to God often includes honoring family.

Beyond ministry, she is a successful entrepreneur, real estate investor, and licensed master cosmetologist, known for ministering to souls from the salon to the pulpit. She is also the Founder of The Throne Room, a ministry dedicated to prayer, healing, and prophetic impartation, where she continues to see God's power transform lives.

Prophetess Catherine's compassion extends beyond the pulpit — she carries a deep passion for the homeless and less fortunate, desiring to build shelters that restore dignity and hope. Known as a quiet benefactor, blessing others in secret, she lives out the truth of Matthew 6:4 (KJV) — "That thine alms may be in secret: and thy Father which seeth in secret himself shall reward thee openly."

Through her prophetic message and ministry, Prophetess Catherine continues to bring hope, supernatural healing, and transformation to those seeking God's presence and truth.

If you want to stay in touch, Prophetess Catherine would love to connect with you, pray with you, and share upcoming events, teachings, and prophetic messages. Stay connected through her official platforms:

Instagram: @Prohetesscathy_

Facebook: Prophetess Catherine Hyatt Ministries

Website: www.TheThroneRoom.co

www.ingramcontent.com/pod-product-compliance
Lightning Source LLC
Chambersburg PA
CBHW051659090426
42736CB00013B/2456